SOFÍA REYES

Stars of Latin Pop   Estrellas del Pop Latino

Written by
Marlene Gutiérrez

Translated by
Alma Patricia Ramirez

Rourke
Educational Media

A Division of
Carson
Dellosa
Education

Before Reading: *Building Background Knowledge and Vocabulary*

Building background knowledge can help children process new information and build upon what they already know. Before reading a book, it is important to tap into what children already know about the topic. This will help them develop their vocabulary and increase their reading comprehension.

Questions and Activities to Build Background Knowledge:

1. Look at the front cover of the book and read the title. What do you think this book will be about?
2. What do you already know about this topic?
3. Take a book walk and skim the pages. Look at the table of contents, photographs, captions, and bold words. Did these text features give you any information or predictions about what you will read in this book?

Vocabulary: *Vocabulary Is Key to Reading Comprehension*

Use the following directions to prompt a conversation about each word.
- Read the vocabulary words.
- What comes to mind when you see each word?
- What do you think each word means?

Vocabulary Words:		Palabras del vocabulario	
• bilingual	• genres	• apasionada	• dueto
• collaborating	• mentor	• bilingüe	• genéros
• duet	• passionate	• colaborar	• mentor

During Reading: *Reading for Meaning and Understanding*

To achieve deep comprehension of a book, children are encouraged to use close reading strategies. During reading, it is important to have children stop and make connections. These connections result in deeper analysis and understanding of a book.

 Close Reading a Text

During reading, have children stop and talk about the following:
- Any confusing parts
- Any unknown words
- Text to text, text to self, text to world connections
- The main idea in each chapter or heading

Encourage children to use context clues to determine the meaning of any unknown words. These strategies will help children learn to analyze the text more thoroughly as they read.

When you are finished reading this book, turn to the next-to-last page for **After Reading Questions** and an **Activity**.

Table of Contents

Tabla de contenido

Surrounded by Song

Rodeada de canciones

Úrsula Sofía Reyes Piñeyro was born in Monterrey, Nuevo León, Mexico. Sofía grew up listening to her grandmother play the piano. Her father was in a band and is a songwriter. Sofía says, "I was always surrounded by music."

• • •

Úrsula Sofía Reyes Piñeyro nació en Monterrey, Nuevo León, México. Sofía creció escuchando a su abuela tocar el piano. Su padre estuvo en una banda y es compositor de canciones. Sofía dice: "Siempre estuve rodeada de música".

United States

Monterrey

Mexico

5

When she was six years old, Sofía started piano lessons. She learned to play the guitar at age 12. Sofía's parents also allowed her to take singing, acting, and modeling lessons. Sofía says, "I owe everything to my parents. They pushed me to pursue my dreams."

• • •

Cuando tenía seis años, Sofía comenzó con lecciones de piano. Aprendió a tocar la guitarra a los 12 años. Los padres de Sofía también le permitieron que tomara clases de canto, actuación y modelaje. Sofía dice: "Todo se lo debo a mis padres. Me impulsaron a realizar mis sueños".

As a young girl, Sofía wrote songs with her dad and made an album with her best friend. She was an actress in the television musical *My Beautiful Anabella* and joined a girl group, TAO. Her first time in a studio, Sofía said, "I realized I wanted to do this forever." Sofía loves most types of music. She performs in many **genres**, including pop, R&B, and reggaetón.

• • •

De pequeña, Sofía escribió canciones con su padre e hizo un álbum con su mejor amigo. Fue actriz en el musical para televisión *Mi Linda Anabella* y se unió al grupo TAO. En su primera vez en un estudio, Sofía dijo: "Me di cuenta de que quería hacer esto por siempre". A Sofía le gustan muchos tipos de música. Ella canta en muchos **géneros**, incluyendo pop, R&B y reguetón.

genres (ZHAHN-ruhz): types or categories of something
géneros (ZHAHN-ruhz): tipos o categorías de algo

Sofía met musician Prince Royce at an awards show. He signed her to his record label when she was 12 years old. She was the first singer to be added to Prince Royce's label. He became her **mentor**.

• • •

Sofía conoció al musico Prince Royce en un evento de premiación. Él la fusionó a su sello discográfico cuando tenía 12 años. Fue la primera cantante que se fusionó al sello discográfico de Prince Royce. Él se convirtió en su **mentor**.

mentor (MEN-tor): a teacher or someone who gives advice
mentor (MEN-tor): un maestro o alguien que da consejos

Prince Royce

Forever Friends

Sofía's friend and mentor Prince Royce changed her life. Sofía says, "I am grateful to Prince Royce for believing in me and helping new artists to accomplish their dreams."

● ● ●

Amigos por siempre

Prince Royce, el amigo y mentor de Sofía cambió su vida. Sofía dice: "Estoy agradecida con Prince Royce por creer en mí y ayudar a los artistas nuevos a cumplir sus sueños".

Making Music

Creando música

Sofía moved to the United States when she was 17 years old. She began performing songs in Spanish and English. She posted songs on YouTube. She says singing in two languages "was a challenge because people were not used to listening to bilingual songs."

● ● ●

Sofá se mudó a Estados Unidos cuando tenía 17 años. Comenzó a cantar canciones en español y en inglés. Subió canciones a YouTube. Ella dice que cantar en dos idiomas "fue un reto porque las personas no estaban acostumbradas a escuchar canciones bilingües".

bilingual (bye-LING-gwuhl): speaking or using two languages
bilingüe (bilingüe): hablar o usar dos idiomas

Spanish-English Swap

Sofía switches between Spanish and English when talking. Sofía also sings the way she speaks. Like Sofía, many people speak two or more languages. Over 60 percent of Latinos in the U.S. are bilingual.

● ● ●

Intercambio español inglés

Sofía cambia entre español e inglés cuando habla. Sofía también canta en la forma en la que habla. Como Sofía, muchas personas hablan dos o más idiomas. Más del 60% de los latinos en Estados Unidos son bilingües.

In 2016, Sofía recorded a **duet** with Prince Royce, *Just Me*. The song hit the number one spot on Billboard's Latin Pop Chart. It was the first time in five years that a female artist reached number one.

• • •

En 2016, Sofía grabó un **dueto** con Prince Royce, *Just Me*. La canción alcanzó el número uno en el Billboard de Pop Latino. Fue la primera vez en cinco años que una artista femenina alcanzaba el número uno.

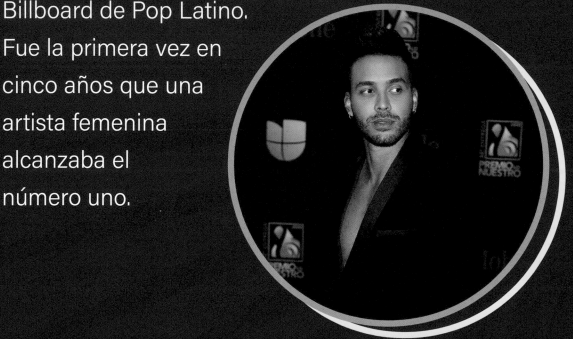

duet (doo-ET): music performed by two singers or instruments

dueto (due-to): música cantada por dos cantantes o tocada por dos instrumentos

Sofía loves **collaborating** with other artists. Sofía worked on the song *R.I.P.* with Anitta and Rita Ora. They performed in three languages: Spanish, English, and Portuguese. The video for *R.I.P.* won Video of the Year at the LOS40 Music Awards.

● ● ●

A Sofía le gusta **colaborar** con otros artistas. Sofía trabajó en la canción *R.I.P.* con Anitta y Rita Ora. Ellas cantaron en tres idiomas: español, inglés y portugués. El video de *R.I.P.* ganó el Video del Año en LOS40 Music Awards.

collaborating (kuh-LAB-uh-rate-ing): working together to accomplish or achieve something
colaborar (co-la-bo-rar): trabajar juntos para lograr o alcanzar algo

Supportive Sisterhood

Sofía is friends with many Latina performers. Sofía says, "We're all team players and help each other." She tells female artists, "I'm here to support you. I'm here to lift you higher."

• • •

Hermandad de apoyo

Sofía es amiga de muchas cantantes latinas. Sofía dice: "Todas jugamos en el mismo equipo y nos ayudamos unas a otras". Ella les dice a las artistas: "Estoy aquí para apoyarte. Estoy aquí para elevarte aún más alto".

Sofía also collaborated with Jason Derulo and De La Ghetto. Their song *1, 2, 3* was a hit! It reached platinum status in over six countries, including the United States. A platinum album means more than one million albums were sold.

• • •

Sofía también colaboró con Jason Derulo y De La Ghetto. Su canción *1, 2, 3* ¡fue un éxito! Alcanzó el estatus de platino en más de seis países, incluidos los Estados Unidos. Un álbum de platino significa que se vendieron más de un millón de álbumes.

Sales, Stars, and Songs

Many people love Sofía and her music! She recorded Mexico's World Cup anthem; *Let's go for the Star*. Sofía has created ads with Jeep, Café Bustelo, Target, Nike, and more.

● ● ●

Ventas, estrellas y canciones

¡Muchas personas aman a Sofía y su música! Ella grabó el himno de la Copa del Mundo de México *Vamos por la Estrella*. Sofía ha creado anuncios para Jeep, Café Bustelo, Target, Nike y más.

Sofía Reyes has performed with other artists like De La Ghetto (left) and Jason Derulo (above).

Sofía Reyes ha colaborado con otros artistas como De La Ghetto (lado izquierdo) y Jason Derulo (arriba).

19

Changing Children's Lives

Cambiando las vidas de los niños

Learning about music and instruments as a child shaped Sofía as an artist. She is **passionate** about giving students a chance to experience music.

● ● ●

Aprender acerca de la música y los instrumentos moldeó a Sofía para convertirse en artista. Ella es **apasionada** cuando se trata de dar a los estudiantes una oportunidad para experimentar la música.

passionate (PASH-uh-nit): feeling very strongly about something

apasionada (a-pa-sio.na-da): un sentimiento muy fuerte acerca de algo

Sofía worked with an after-school program to create the video for her song *So Beautiful*. She remains in contact with kids from the video.

• • •

Sofía trabajó con un programa para después de la escuela para crear el video para la canción *So Beautiful*. Ella sigue en contacto con los niños del video.

Sofía helps State Farm Insurance support music education in schools. She also worked on a program for Latino kids called Voices with Dedication. She chose five students and gave them each $10,000 to pursue music. Sofía says, "It's helped me a lot to help others."

• • •

Sofía ayuda a State Farm Insurance a apoyar la educación musical en las escuelas. También trabajó en un programa para niños latinos llamado Voces con dedicación. Eligió a cinco estudiantes y les dio $10,000 a cada uno para continuar con la música. Sofía dice: "Ayudar a otras personas me ha ayudado mucho".

Sofía wants to be thought of as someone who "changed the world in a positive way, inspired people to follow their dreams."

• • •

Sofía quiere que se le recuerde como alguien que "cambió al mundo en una manera positiva, inspiró a las personas a realizar sus sueños".

Children's Charities

Sofía has been a Goodwill Ambassador for the Special Olympic World Games. She raises money for children with cancer. She loves helping children any way she can!

• • •

Caridades para los niños

Sofía ha sido Embajadora de Buena Voluntad para los Juegos Mundiales de las Olimpiadas Especiales. Recauda dinero para los niños con cáncer. ¡Le gusta ayudar a los niños en todas las maneras que pueda!

Sofía has followed her dreams. She has worked with other musicians. She has offered opportunities to children who love music. Sofía is working to change the world. How will your dreams make the world better?

• ● •

Sofía ha realizado sus sueños. Ha trabajado con otros músicos. Ha ofrecido oportunidades a los niños que aman la música. Sofía está trabajando para cambiar al mundo. ¿Cómo harán tus sueños que el mundo sea mejor?

Index

After-Reading Questions

1. How was music an important part of Sofía's childhood?

2. What were some things that happened during Sofía's life that led to her becoming famous?

3. How has being bilingual influenced Sofía's career?

4. How does Sofía feel about other female musicians?

5. What are some of the things Sofía has done to help children?

Activity

Sofía has collaborated with friends, family, and other artists for most of her life. You can work with others to create many things, including music, art, food, clothing, and more. Think of a person or people you would like to collaborate with. What will you do with them? What talents and skills will you each bring to the collaboration? Write or sketch out a plan for what you will make, and then put your plan into action to create something wonderful!

Índice

Preguntas para después de la lectura

1. ¿Cómo se convirtió la música en una parte importante en la vida de Sofía cuando estaba creciendo?

2. ¿Cuáles son algunas de las cosas que sucedieron en la vida de Sofía que la llevaron a ser famosa?

3. ¿Cómo influyó el ser bilingüe en la carrera de Sofía?

4. ¿Qué piensa Sofía acerca de otras cantantes?

5. ¿Cuáles son algunas de las cosas que Sofía ha hecho para ayudar a los niños?

Actividad

Sofía ha colaborado con amigos, familiares y otros artistas la mayor parte de su vida. Puedes trabajar con otras personas para crear muchas cosas, incluidas la música, el arte, la comida, la ropa y más. Piensa en una persona o personas con las que te gustaría colaborar. ¿Qué harías con ellos? ¿Qué talentos y destrezas traería cada uno a la colaboración? Escribe o traza un plan para lo que harás, y después ¡pon tu plan a trabajar para crear algo maravilloso!

About the Author
Sobre la autora

Jolene Gutiérrez also believes in the power of music and works as a teacher-librarian at a school in Denver, Colorado. Connecting students with books and sharing information are some of Jolene's favorite things. Learn more about Jolene, her writing, and her dreams at **www.jolenegutierrez.com**.

• • •

Jolene Gutiérrez también cree en el poder de la música y trabaja como maestra y bibliotecaria en una escuela en Denver, Colorado. Conectar a los estudiantes con libros y compartir información son algunas de las cosas favoritas de Jolene. Obtén más información sobre Jolene, su escritura y sus sueños en **www.jolenegutierrez.com**.

Quote source: Calvario, Liz. "Sofia Reyes on Her Breakthrough Year and Finding Love (Exclusive)." Entertainment Tonight. September 25, 2018: https://www.etonline.com/sofia-reyes-on-her-breakthrough-year-and-finding-her-voice-in-the-latin-music-industry-exclusive ; Entertainment Tonight. "The Sofia Reyes Story: My Life As A Latina." YouTube. Last modified September 25, 2018. https://www.youtube.com/watch?v=zwk5T-pa6-s ; iHeartRadio. "Sofia Reyes - Artist Stories - Interview (2016) - Parts 1 and 2." YouTube. September 6, 2016 ; Savage, Mark. "Sofia Reyes: Meet Mexico's Multilingual Pop Sensation." BBC News. April 4, 2019: https://www.bbc.com/news/entertainment-arts-47799358. "Sofia Reyes- Biography." Warner Records Press. June 25, 2020. https://press.warnerrecords.com/wp-content/uploads/2019/06/Sofia-Reyes-BIO.pdf.

PHOTO CREDITS: Cover: ©Oscar Gonzalez/ZUMA Press / Newscom; page 3: ©Action Press/ZUMA Press / Newscom(top); page 3: ©JLJ/ZOJ/JLN Photography/WENN / Newscom(bottom); page 4: ©diegocarrales / Shutterstock; page 6: ©Denis Val / Shutterstock; page 7: ©JLN Photography/WENN.com / Newscom; page 9: ©JIM RUYMEN/UPI / Newscom; page 11: ©Alberto E. Tamargo/Sipa USA / Newscom; page 13: ©Eyepix/Sipa USA / Newscom; page 14: ©Alberto E. Tamargo/Sipa USA / Newscom; page 15: ©JIM RUYMEN/UPI / Newscom; page 17: ©Ian West/ZUMA Press / Newscom; page 18: ©Alberto E. Tamargo/Sipa USA / Newscom; page 19: ©Alberto E. Tamargo/Sipa USA / Newscom; page 21: ©JLN Photography/WENN.com / Newscom: page 22: ©Tinseltown / Shutterstock; page 23: ©Kathy Hutchins / Shutterstock; page 25: ©Kamira / Shutterstock; page 27: ©Featureflash Photo Agency / Shutterstock

Library of Congress PCN Data

Sofia Reyes / Jolene Gutiérrez
(Stars of Latin Pop)
ISBN 978-1-73164-334-6 (hard cover)
ISBN 978-1-73164-298-1 (soft cover)
ISBN 978-1-73164-366-7 (e-Book)
ISBN 978-1-73164-398-8 (ePub)
Library of Congress Control Number: 2020945044

Rourke Educational Media
Printed in the United States of America
01-3502011937

Edited by: Madison Capitano
Cover design by: Michelle Rutschilling
Interior design by: Book Buddy Media